Anyway,
I Reach

Kristina Mahr

For love,
and those
who still believe in it.

A NOTE

This is my third collection, and as such, I hoped to have
discovered some overarching meaning to it all.

And, I believe, I have –

it all happened so that I could write about it.

And so that you could read it, if you find you need to.

As ever, these poems are displayed in the order that I
wrote them, with hope beside hopelessness, love beside
loss, because this life is a messy business.

Messy and wonderful and mine.

This Mountain

I climbed this mountain,

I climbed this mountain,

it took me two years,

but I climbed this mountain.

I only wish it had taken more
　　than one small push
　　　　to fall back to the bottom of it.

It Has Taken Some Time

It has taken some time
to not see myself
as you saw me —

as someone easy to walk away from.

It has taken some time for me
to not want to walk away from me, too.

Stuck with It

I limp through life
on a broken heart.
It is slow-going.
I am careful
and I am scared
and I do not yet know
if I can be repaired.
If I have the parts I need in stock
or if I'll have to wait for someone else
to bring them.
Or neither, maybe it's neither,
maybe this is it for me.
Maybe you were it for me.
One time use,
buyer beware,
you broke it and
you returned it and

I

am

stuck with it.

Not Sorry

Sometimes I think about
calling you up to say
I'm sorry
for wringing us out like a washcloth
and collecting all of these words
in a bucket
before dumping them out
for everyone to see.

But then I think,
they're a little bit beautiful.

But then I think,
we were a little bit beautiful.

And I am not sorry
that I found beauty
in the wreck you left my heart.

What a Mess

I still wear it on my sleeve
even though I'm not sure anyone
wants to see it anymore.
I know it isn't pretty.
I know it has holes and cracks
and it drips blood all over the place
and I know I should probably
keep it hidden in my chest
or at least cover it,
at least wrap it,
at least pretend to be
embarrassed by it,
what a mess,
what a goddamn mess,
I guess I should be embarrassed by it.

(But I'm not.)

I am still never
    anything
        but proud of it.

Ending

It is a coming home,
and it is a salvaging,
and it is a hope,
a hope for more.

I remind myself of this
on the days
it only feels like an ending.

All the Same Stars

I saw all the same stars tonight,
all the same stars tonight,
they just didn't

        shine

          as bright.

In Earnest Now

Winter's here in earnest now,
and I don't think of you anymore.
Your name doesn't cross my mind
as my boots crunch through ice and snow,
and I don't flinch
when someone else holds
my gloved hand.
There are ice skaters out on the pond,
and I know that once
you asked me to go with you,
but I don't think of it while I watch them.
And it's nearly February,
which is the month before March,
which precedes April,
which is so very near to May,
and it's May when you stopped loving me,
it's May when we last spoke,
it's May when I last felt
anything,
anything,
but none of that means anything
because

it's winter here in earnest now,
and I
don't think of you
anymore.

Discovered

I have been discovered before.
Flag planted through the heart of me,
claimed,
name changed to sweetheart,
baby,
honey.
I have been taught a new language,
one of hand squeezes
and laughter
and silences that lasted days.
And I have tried,
I have tried,
to be glad for it all,
to feel like I was lost
before I was found,
to feel like I am more now
because someone
else
has me.
(I have tried.)
But instead I find I miss
when I was wild,
when I was free,
when I
    was
        mine.

Close Enough

I always wanted to be an astronaut,
but I sit on my lawn
and I look at the stars,
and I feel like that's close enough.

And I always wanted to own a farm,
but I pick apples in a nearby orchard
and I have a dog that gallops like a horse,
and I feel like that's close enough.

Mostly I always wanted to be in love,
but I fell in love with you
and you didn't love me back,
and —

no, in this,
there's no such thing
    as close
        enough.

Steel Trap

I haven't forgotten,
I don't want you to think I've forgotten.
(Any of it.)
Steel trap up here,
can't slip out,
can't escape
a damn bit of it.
I keep it all,
though every other day
I want to lose the good
and every other day
I want to lose the bad,
no,
I keep it all,
steel trap up here.
You know what I mean,
do you know what I mean.
I cannot lose us
no matter that
I have
already
lost us.

Less Frequent, Less Urgent

I have a list of things to tell you
if we ever talk again.
I used to add to it every night,
but now it's less frequent,
less urgent,
it's less
I miss you
I miss you
I miss you
and more
I read a book I think you'd like
and
I heard a joke you might find funny
and
I heard a laugh in a crowd today
that sounded just like yours
and I started pushing through people
and searching for you
before my mind caught up with my elbows,
my feet,
my heart.

It's less frequent,
less urgent.

But I guess it all means the same thing.

No

No.
No, I was not happy.
Loving you was like
standing on an iceberg
getting smaller by the second,
and maybe sometimes
you would come
and stand beside me,
but even then,
it was cold,
and even then,
I was afraid
of how much water
surrounded us
on all four sides.
Loving you was like
sinking,
like
shrinking,
like
drowning.
No, I was not happy.

(But every now and then, you held my hand.)

(You don't do that anymore.)

Prey

I root for the mouse
to get away,
but that's not to say
I want the hawk to starve.
It's a matter of relating, you see.
I have been the thing
torn to shreds,
but I have never been
the thing that tears.
I have no talons,
I have never needed
to watch something smaller than me
bleed.
Did you need to,
(did you want to.)
What was it you were hungry for,
(what was it you were starving for.)

I am torn,
and I am bleeding,
but I guess
it wasn't
me.

Quiet

We are quiet,
but we are not out
of things to say.
I have turned the way you left
into poetry now
because nobody has ever told me
what to do with
all of these words
left in boxes
in my attic.
Collecting dust
and pounding on the ceiling.
So I write them
and we are
anything but quiet
in them,
do you hear us,
we are loud in them,
which is good because
we are not out
of things to say,
or perhaps I mean
that I am not.

I think maybe that you are.

I think maybe that's the saddest part of all.

From the Outside

From the outside
I am inside,
where else would I be.
Can't leave this skin,
can't shed it,
must be in here,
must be.
My eyes are windows,
yeah,
but they're all fogged up,
it's cold in here,
can't see in,
can't find me.
I am kicking in walls,
I am screaming,
I am screaming,
but the question is from where.

Because
from the outside
I am inside.

From the inside

I

am

gone.

Waiting

You said you had to go,
and I waited,
and I waited.

You left,
and I waited,
and I waited.

You are still gone,
and I'm waiting,
and I'm waiting.

(I would have come with you.)

I have only ever been

waiting

for you

to ask.

Freedom

I call it freedom now too,
it just took me a little longer.
Caged dog caged so long
it takes a day and a half for it to realize
someone forgot to shut the door.
No, I knew, though,
I knew I could run.
Could and should,
I just never knew about
would.
They all say love's soft,
but then why don't its bars bend,
why is there no give.
(Only take, only take.)
These are only more questions
you won't answer.
Add them to the list
before you crumple it up
and burn it.
Beneath *why*,
beneath *why*.
Keep it short,
all you need to write
is yet another
why.

More than Enough

I think we were less
than what we should have been.
But that doesn't mean
we weren't more than enough
to matter.

Sometimes I Think

Sometimes I think my whole life
has been me pounding
on the insides of my windows,
waiting for someone to care enough
to stop and look inside.
Like I've gone missing
and I'm yelling, "I'm here, I'm here,"
but nobody knows to look for me,
everyone thinks it's just the wind, calling,
just the creaks in this old house, falling.
Sometimes someone pauses and I think,
this is it, this is it, this is it,
but they never look close enough
to see me.

Sometimes I think my whole life
has been me wanting
to be seen.

Sometimes I think my whole life
has been me clinging tight to the belief
that there's something here worth seeing.

You Are There

He was a new layer of paint,
but you are the walls,
you are the plaster,
you are the beams.

He peels off,
I scrub him off,
I scrape him off –

and you are there,

you are there,

you are there.

Yours

Love gives you wings.

(I don't want wings.)

I just want a hand in mine.

(I want it to be yours.)

I just want arms around me.

(I want them to be yours.)

I just want more than to only ever be my own.

(I want to be yours.)

Voicemail

It's late now,
and I'm just calling to say I miss you.

It's cold in here,
and I have nowhere warm to tuck my feet.
I'm scared to close my eyes,
scared I'll dream you going,
scared I'll dream you here.

My phone is pressed against my ear
like I used to press it there
to hear your voice,
to hear you breathing,
to make it like you were here with me,
but now all I hear
is the echo of my own voice saying

it's late now

and I'm just calling to say

I miss you.

One Us

In the history of the world,

there have been

are

will be

so many of us,

but there

has only ever been

will only ever be

one us.

Missing

I've been so worried about missing
all of the ends of your stories,
all of the middles,
all of the new beginnings,
that it took me til now to realize
how many of mine
you're missing.

I wish I was there,
I do,
I do,
but more than that I think
that you'll wish
that you
were here.

This Heart of Mine

You always knew
what this heart of mine was,
and I think that's why
I can't believe
you didn't know
you were breaking it.

2016

That was the year I loved you,
I say,
and I say it like someone
who knows better now.
Me, I learn from my mistakes,
but you weren't a mistake,
I have called you many things,
many things,
but I have never called you a mistake.
(I have called you lost.)
(I have called you mine.)
If I know anything better now,
it's that other people have hands
that open just as easily as they close,
and somehow mine
only know how to close.
So I keep that in mind.
And I tell people
that was the year I loved you,
if they ask where I was,
what I was doing.
I tell people that was the year
I learned
that there are other people
for other people
and there is only

you

for me.

Warning Label

Careful or
you'll cut yourself on me, look
I know what I am.
I should come with
a warning label,
beware of sharp edges,
objects in front of you
may be closer
than they appear,
this slope,
this slope
is slippery.
Maybe these poems
are my warning label,
here, read them,
go ahead and read them all.
They'll tell you why
I have sharp edges.
They'll tell you why
I stand farther away
than I'd like.
They'll tell you why
it takes me a long time
to decide to fall,
but that when I do,
I
don't
stop.

What's Best for Me

I hate that you think
you did
what's best for me.

I hate that you think
you have any idea
in all of the world
what's best for me.

But mostly I hate
that I can't get over
thinking you're
what's best for me.

Peace

I think peace

is looking back and knowing

I did it all

for love.

Detonated

I call it folding
because it sounds
more elegant than
collapsing.
I stand tall
because my bones
and my pride
require it of me,
but inside,
I have been
detonated.
I pick through the rubble
but I can't find anything here
worth saving.
I guess that makes sense because
even before
you lit the fuse,
you couldn't find anything here

worth

saving.

Brick

I am building with brick now.

Something beautiful,
something lasting.

(You were straw.)

(You were sticks.)

You were
gone
gone
gone
the very first time
a storm
blew
through.

I'm Convinced

I want you like
a child
wants to touch every fragile thing
up and down the aisles
of every store,
and I need you like
a wildflower
needs rain
in the middle of a drought,
and I'm convinced,
I'm convinced,
I love you like
nobody

has ever

loved anything

before.

It's Not Easy

It's not easy

loving someone

who isn't here,

but it's easier

than figuring out

how to stop.

Now I Wonder

He looks at me
the way you looked at me.

(I loved the way you looked at me.)

But now I wonder if it's only
how people look at me
when they know
    they're going
        to leave.

The Trouble Is

The trouble is,
they see it in my eyes.

The trouble is,
they know

I'm still

in love with you.

The Reasons Why

I am looking under rocks,
and I am checking behind doors,
and I am slamming the heel of my hand
against the side of my head,
over and over and over
again,
and I am trying,
I am trying,
I am trying to find
the reasons why
I used to love
myself
but I think
that they
may have been
another thing
you took with you
when
you went.

So Much Easier

He scared easily,
is the story I tell about you.
Oh him,
he said things,
yes,
he said things,
good things,
but he didn't mean them.
He wrote checks with his words
he couldn't cash with his hands.
If there was a choice
between staying and going,
he'd always go,
always,
it's so much easier
to buy something new
than to fix
what you already
have.

It's so much easier.

Unless you're the thing
that wasn't
worth
fixing.

A Day

Give me a day,
one day,
we'll sit side by side
in your living room
and we'll see
what we
can make of us.

We'll reminisce,
we'll make believe,
or maybe we'll make it
real.

Give me a day,
one day,
and at least maybe I can see
what you saw
that didn't seem worth
another
day.

Extraordinary

We will be extraordinary,
the two of us,
you in your life
and me in mine,
I have no doubt
we will be extraordinary.

So just think
      what we could have been
            together.

A Bit

I hate that you know where I live.
It means that when a car pulls into my driveway,
my heart leaps
because it knows it could be you.
Could be, yes, could be,
but it takes a bit for it to remember that
it won't be.
A bit, I say a bit,
like a second, maybe six, maybe twelve,
in any case,
enough for it to hurt,
no, it doesn't take much,
doesn't take a lot,
takes hardly anything these days
for it to hurt.
I am tired of the hurt,
and I'm not ashamed to say it,
either of it,
that I hurt
or that I'm tired.
This is what there is now,
this,
this is all there is now,
this,
but it'll be done
    in just
        a bit.

Love Doesn't Leave

Love doesn't leave.

Either it stays

or it was never

really

there.

Charlie Brown

It is raining in my living room and
in my bedroom and
in this open field during everyone else's
sunshine day
and I guess I'm Charlie Brown now
with a rain cloud over my head,
and I guess you're Lucy now,
ripping the football away every time
I'm brave enough to try to kick it,
and is this what you wanted for your life,
is this what you always wanted for your life,
to look back some day and know
and know
and know
that you broke somebody's heart
this way.
(It's not that you broke it.)
(It's that you broke it this way.)

Is this what you wanted.

Because you told me
    what you wanted
        was me.

How Not To

If the question is
do I care,
the answer is
I am still trying
to learn from you
how not to.

Believe

There are things

we can't see

that we can only choose

to believe in,

and to me,

you are one of

those things.

Echoes

This is what I am now.
Pen clutched in one hand,
your picture held tight in the other.
This, this, I am the ash left
in the ash tray
where something
used to
burn.
My fingertips are erasers,
my tongue is a scythe,
I step up to the intercom and ask
if anyone
has seen
my heart.
Please bring it to the front, if you have.
Dead or alive,
dead or alive,
I just want to be more
than empty.

(It echoes in here.)

Your name,
your name,
your name.

Too

There is so much power
in the word too, in

I feel that too,
I want that too,
I love you too,

like you
    are not
        alone in this.

You don't love me anymore.

But if you could just say
you miss me too,
I might not feel so
alone in this.

Pride

My pride looks different than yours.

Yours is in pretending nothing hurts.

Mine is in knowing I tried everything,

everything,

everything

to prevent this from being something

that hurts.

Twelve Steps

I'm in a twelve step program
to get over you where
step one is
delete your number and
step two is
unmemorize your number and
step three is
stop dreaming you and
step four is
stop wanting you and
step five is
stop missing you and
step six is
find someone new and
step seven is
stop pretending he's you and
step eight is
fine remember you fine but
step nine is
I have to remember the bad and
step ten is
I have to remember the hurt and
step eleven is
I can't keep doing this and
step twelve is
keep trying keep trying keep trying
because I have no choice
but to
keep doing this.

A Thing That Goes

Sometimes I think that life
is much too short
and far too beautiful
to spend another moment
chasing after the things that go,
but then I think
our time together
was much too short
and far too beautiful
to let it be
a thing
that goes.

At Last, At Last

Like it has been night now for months
that have snuck into years
and the sun stretches into the sky,
at last, at last,

so too am I stretching,
at last, at last,
to fill the empty space
you left.

The Only Place

This is the only place I still write you.
Here,
between
the four walls of this page,
I write you love letters and
loss letters and
forgiveness letters and
I miss you letters,
and it's the only place,
the only place,
the only place

where I still write you

and where I still write me

as not just you

and not just me

but us.

Change It Back

I just keep thinking,
I just keep thinking —

I hated that you could change your mind
so suddenly, so easily,
but now, knowing that you can, I think —

at least this means
you can change
it back.

This Isn't a Love Poem

This isn't a love poem.
(I don't write those.)
No, this is about the time in fourth grade
when the teacher spelled my name wrong
on the board,
and I didn't want to say anything,
but my best friend stood up and said,
"She spells it with a K."
It's about the time my dog brought me
his favorite toy when I was crying on the couch.
It's about the time the boy I loved
held my hand in a theater
when the man on the screen knew
he was breaking that woman's heart,
and I think it's because he knew
he was breaking my heart.
It's about leap day,
and it's about Halley's comet,
and it's about the every hundred years
when the Queen of the Andes blooms,
and it's about things that are rare
and things that are beautiful
and it
is about
miracles.

(I guess it's a love poem after all.)

Love

Love is a grey wolf,
a Siberian tiger,
a killer whale —

it is beautiful,
but the closer I get to it,
the more terrified I am.

Save Me

I let the water run hot,
let the glass fog up,
write "save me,"
write nothing but "save me,"
underline it twice,
cross it out,
write it again.

I don't know how you don't see it.

I don't know how
   you pretend
      you don't
         see it.

Arson

You won't ever find me
where you're looking,
if you're looking,
if you're thinking you might want
to think about looking.
No, I'm not there,
I haven't been there,
I won't go back there.
They think I'm arson,
try me as a felony,
sentence me to life and
don't listen to my appeals.
My appeals, my appeals
wailing,
my appeals
howling,
my appeals that are only ever this —
I lit a match in the middle of a forest
because I was cold and couldn't see
where I was going.
I swear I didn't know
    it would cause
        all this.

This

I think
it has always
been this:

you, looking
at the road,
at the mountains,
at the moon;

me,
only ever
looking
at you.

Not Tonight

If even a broken clock
is right twice a day,
I wonder how often
a broken heart is.

I think not tonight,
as it's calling your name.

I think not tonight,
as it's wishing you,
wishing you
back.

Maybe it'll be right
another time,
another day,
but I don't think
    it's right
        tonight.

He Doesn't Realize

He asks me about you,
though he doesn't know it.
He thinks he's just asking
why I don't trust him,
why I won't let him in,
where my thoughts go
when I'm staring out the window.

He thinks he's just asking me to love him.

He doesn't realize
    he's also asking me
        to stop loving you.

Complicated

We make love so complicated

when all we really ever need

is to not

feel

alone in it.

I'm Sorry

I visit our grave twice a week,
I'm sorry,
twice a day,
I'm sorry,
I also sleep there every night.
I spend an hour smashing
the tombstone to bits
and another hour gluing
it back together.
I plant flowers and I let
the weeds grow wild
and strangle them.
I trace the letters of our names and mine
has deeper grooves than yours,
I trace the beginning and end dates and mine
ends on a different day than yours.

Our ghosts keeps me company,
so I am not alone.

We are laughing, and we are happy,
and I have never
                    felt more
                              alone.

To Life

I want to love you to life,
I want to love you to life.

(But I cannot see you anymore.)

And Only Ever You

I do not understand how
yesterday
I was not enough
and the day before
I was too much,
when I am me
and only ever me
and only ever me.

It makes me think
the problem is less with me
and only ever me
and only ever me

and perhaps

more

with you.

(And only ever you.)

(And only ever you.)

From the Sparrows

I decide each day
if I want to sit on this ledge
or dangle from it.
That's it, those are the options,
I cannot leave the ledge.
But I can sit
or I can dangle,
and I make that small choice
every morning.
It's better than nothing —
I used to only ever dangle.
I used to hang from my fingertips
while the crows called out my name.
Now some days I still dangle,
when I want to feel the strain of my muscles
and the pound of my heart,
but most days I climb up and sit
on this narrow little ledge
and I rest my head against the wall
and close my eyes and realize
that only some of the calls are from crows.

(The rest are coming from the sparrows.)

Unsure

I write everything
as though you're reading it,
but I'll write this
as though you're not —

I'm not sure I ever loved you,
but I'm just as unsure
if I'll ever
stop.

Everything

Sometimes I wish
I'd told you less,
but mostly I wish
I'd told you

everything.

From the Beginning

I have loved you this long,
and precisely this long,
and just as long as this —

from the beginning.

(That's all there is.)

Pulse

There is no pulse on this page
until I put it there.
Each word is like the spike of an EKG,
like *live*,
like *live*,
like *please live*.

(I am desperate for a heartbeat.)

Are these words enough.

No,
how about these,
no,
how about these.

Are these something you might live for.

Are they something I might live for.

I hide my hands behind my back
because to others it's just ink,
but to me, but to me,
it's only ever blood from pages
I couldn't bring to life.

The Way That I Hold On

It is either my greatest weakness
or my greatest strength, this —

the way

that I

hold on.

Every Night Ends

Every night ends,
no matter how you hope it never will,
    no matter how you fear it never will.

It will,
and when it does,
you have the day to see what survives,
    you have the day to see that you've survived.

More

Neither of us was wrong
for wanting more.
Not me,
for wanting more with you.
And not you,
for wanting more

than

me.

Do You See

I want you in my dreams
and I want you out of them.
I am as tired
of closing my eyes and seeing you
as I am
of living my life and not.

My tongue is bitten
clean in half,
but that doesn't stop my heart
from begging it to speak.

What would it say,
what would it say,
what is it pleading
bleeding
to have said —

you gave me away.

Do you know,
do you understand,
do you see.

You had me forever,
and you gave
                me
                   away.

Puppet

I put my heart on strings and I say dance,
dance I say,
I say dance.

With him,
no, not him,
what are you doing,
not him.

I tug desperately this way and that,
but my heart is no puppet,
and I am no master.

My heart says him.

My heart has never
    said anything
        but him.

I Know

There is going to be more than this,
and I know it doesn't feel like it.
I know you thought his name
was in the title
instead of just a chapter heading,
and I know the word *'just'*
has no place in any of this.

I know and I know and
there is no part of me
that does not know.

It's just that none of this is easy.

(I know that, too.)

And I just wanted you to know

I know.

Maybe

Maybe you loved
the way that I moved
more than where I went.

Maybe you loved
the sound of my voice
more than the things I said.

Maybe you loved
the pound of my heart
more than what it held.

Maybe you never loved me.

Maybe
            you never
                        knew me.

My Heart Breaks Here

My heart breaks here,
that's all I know about here.

I draw an X on the map,
I try another town,
I try another town.

I never stay long,
just long enough to stare
at a new ceiling
in a new house,
just long enough to know
that there are cracks here, too.

So I draw another X.

I try another town.

(I try every town but yours.)

Because I already know
    my heart
        breaks there.

Nothing

You make me happy,
I'm sorry, I mean
you made me happy.
And I'm not worth the price
you paid for me now,
what price did you pay for me,
I know what price I paid for you.
My feet don't step right and
my eyes don't close right and
my skin doesn't fit right
is the price I paid for you.
A body that's mine,
that's only ever been mine,
and now it doesn't feel like it,
is the price I paid for you.
And that's to say nothing of my heart.
That's to say nothing of my heart,
let's say nothing of my heart,
I will say nothing of my heart,
because nothing
is now all
that it says.

Petals

He is careful to take the thorns off
so that he gives me only petals.

But I don't know —

I kind

of want

to bleed.

Privilege

It is a privilege to miss you
because it means
I once
had you.

Easiest Thing

Easiest thing I ever did, losing you.

I just stood there while you left,
just like that,
I just stood there.

And then, and then,
I threw my body at the closed door,
I banged my head against it,
I kicked it,
I pounded on it until both wrists broke,
and then I kept right on pounding on it,
kept pounding on it,
I'm still pounding on it.

Easiest thing I ever did, losing you.

Hardest thing I ever did, being
                              left
                                   by you.

Stolen

I loved our stolen moments,
until you started stealing

them

from me.

Little Victories

I check the days off on a calendar
like I'm counting down to something,
but I'm counting up.
I can't stand the thought of
forever without you and
I can't stand the thought of
a year
a month
a week
without you,
but I can get through a day,
so I check the days off —
each one a little victory
in a war
I was afraid
I'd already
lost.

Only Ever

Look, you're not
the boy who never called or
the boy who made me cry or
the boy who broke my heart.

When I tell our story
to somebody new,
you're only ever the boy
I fell head over heels
in love with.

The Hardest Truths

Some of the hardest truths you will find are that

what you prioritize
will not always prioritize you

and

what you want
will not always want you

and

what you love
will not always love you

and

you have to decide
what you'll do with this.

Gulf

Your truth looks different than mine,
but it doesn't mean that either is untrue.
It only means that
the one cushion between us
on this couch
is a gulf neither of us
know
how to cross.

It only means that
it is a river and we can't swim;
it is the sky and we can't fly.

It only means that
this'll be hard.

But it doesn't mean

it can't

be done.

The Wind

I used to think that love was the wind,
and I was just waiting to be carried.
I'd zip up my jacket and pull up grass,
throwing it in the air to see
which direction love would come from,
and I'd wait.
I'd sit, eventually, because my bones are less young
than they might otherwise be,
and I'd pull up some more grass
and throw it in the air again
and it would fall on my hair
and on my shoulders
and on my lap
like confetti,
and I'd wonder if this was worth celebrating.
This waiting.
When I stood up and started walking,
it fell from my hair and my shoulders and my lap
to the ground,
and this,
I agreed, was worth celebrating.
That I stood up.
That I stopped waiting and started

walking.

Nothing Uncertain

There is nothing uncertain about this.
There was everything uncertain about that,
but this, no, this is not a weatherman
doing his best two weeks out, no,
this is the center of a hurricane
where there can be no doubt.
Two weeks ago, they thought
maybe it could strike here,
but maybe it'll strike there,
but also it's possible it won't strike anywhere,
but now, the windows are all breaking,
the water's to my knees,
the wind keeps drowning out my voice.
There is nothing uncertain about this.

That it's here, now,
and that it'll be over, soon.

That it'll be me
and the glass
and the water,
and still,
you won't be able to
hear
my voice.

Daylight Savings

I was going to watch the sun rise.

There's an old friend I've been meaning to call,
and my dad's been waiting for me
to go through my old things.

I wanted to walk barefoot in the sand for a while,
just to feel it,
just to remember it,
and I thought I might try yoga.

I wanted to note the exact time
the first star shone through the darkness,
and I wanted to know which star it was.

I was finally going to get over you.

I was, I swear I was.

But we lost an hour today, and so
I'm sorry to say,
I still love you.

Cause of Death

Nobody can determine cause of death.
Maybe that cut,
maybe that slice,
maybe this one,
maybe that one.
Maybe all of them,
maybe it was all of them combined.
That time you didn't call, plus
that time you didn't write, plus
that time I didn't answer
when you asked me what I wanted.
(You.)
(I wanted you.)
A hundred thousand hairline fractures,
but I think I could have lived with them,
I think we could have lived with them,
I think we could have
                    loved
                              with them.
(But I understand why you didn't want to.)

March and You

In like a lion, out like a lamb,
they say about March
and I say about you.

In like "I want to be with you,"
out like "this is just too hard."

While I'm still standing here,
still standing here,

still roaring

at the top of

my lungs.

I Don't Feel It

I don't know how to give up,
when to give up,
how the hell am I supposed to know
if this is the last straw or if
there's more to come.
If the camel's back is broken
or just bruised.

(If my heart is broken or just bruised.)

Is there going to be a sign,
some sort of sign,
am I going to feel it in my bones.

(I don't feel it in my bones.)

Tell me how you knew
it was time
to give up.

I'm Describing This Poorly

It's like there are fire ants swimming in my veins,
and I just woke up in a country
where no one understands a word I say.
Like I had two hands
and now I only have one.
Like I've forgotten all of the words
and the title
and the melody
of the song that used to save me.
Like there's somewhere else I'm supposed to be.
Someone else I'm supposed to be.
Like two roads diverged in a yellow wood,
and I chose wrong,
I always choose wrong,
except this time I was sure I chose right.

I'm sorry, I'm describing this poorly.

My heart is broken.

That's all I was trying to say.

Condemned

Hurt keeps billowing out of me
like it's smoke
and I'm a house on fire.
The truth is, it's the opposite,
I'm the opposite,
nothing's on fire anymore.
I am charred walls and things
someone once treasured
that now crumble at the slightest touch.
I am caution-taped,
condemned,
one strong breeze and what's left of me
will fall.

Hurt swirls and dips and disappears
just before it reaches the stars.

And somebody walks by and says,
"I wonder what they'll build here next."

"I wonder if it'll be beautiful."

Wasted

I don't have a clock in my room,
but I feel the seconds ticking by all the same.

My heart is counting down for me,
each beat another grain
of fallen sand.

Do you feel it.

Do you feel the wasted grains,
the way we're not getting that one back
or that one back
or that one back.

The way we're never getting any of this back.

Look, whichever one is coming next
and coming next
and coming next —

they're only wasted if I'm not with you.

Decisions

Love is magic
and wonder
and a series of decisions.

What I'm saying is
love is nothing
if you don't
decide
to stay.

Just Wait

He said I had
don't leave me eyes,
and I thought,
just wait'll
you see
my heart.

I Wish It

I have this in me,
painted straight down the center of me,
like Hester with her scarlet A,
I have
I am never getting over this
where everyone can read it.
I step up to the scaffold
as everyone whispers and shakes their heads,
as you're nowhere to be found,
and I hold my head up high.
When they ask me for your name,
I never say it,
I never say it,
they ask me, but
I never say it.

But I think it,
and I hold it,
and I wish it.

I think it and
I hold it and
    even
        after
           all
                this time

I wish it.

Anyway

She had flowers in her hair
and he had leaving in his shoes,
everybody knew it,
and deep down, she did too.

But she loved him anyway.

Tragedy and Solace

It is a tragedy that
what I had to give
wasn't enough for you

and

it is a tragedy that
what you had to give
wasn't enough for me

but

that we gave each other
all that we could
is where I find
my solace.

Not Here

I am probably over hills,
most likely through some deserts,
certainly beneath oceans.
I am a pilgrimage,
an odyssey,
I'm whatever's beyond the edge of a map.
I can't find me, can you find me, can you find me.

(Are you looking.)

I am hidden though not hiding,
I am gone though trying so hard not to go.

I am here, I swear,
I am here.

It isn't that
I wish I was not here, it's just
my here is not your here,
and so,

I wish
I was
not here.

What It Will Be

It was what it was, they say,
as I try to change what was.

It is what it is, they say,
as I try to run from what is.

It will be what it will be, they say,
as I am terrified of what will be, because

I cannot change that you left
and
I cannot change that you're gone
and
I am terrified
I cannot change
that you're never
coming
back.

Which One of Us

I don't know which one of us broke it,

but I know which one of us decided

that it wasn't

worth

fixing.

Barbed Wire

I have barbed wire on my tongue,
so every word I say comes out in pieces,
shredded,
ugly,
every word is sure there won't be more
to follow it.
How could more follow it
when I'm gargling blood,
when it's dripping down my throat,
when you don't want to hear it.

(You don't want to hear it.)

I try to clean them up,
I try to strip away the edges,
I swallow all of the blood.

I say I love you,
and I make it soft,
and still,
you
don't want
to hear it.

He Decided

He decided
I didn't need
any answers.

(I am trying not to need any answers.)

Last Stand

I imagine it guns blazing,
making its last stand,
knowing it doesn't stand a chance
but refusing to be taken alive.
It's scarred, it's bloodied, it's been fighting
for years now.
It's been screaming
never surrender,
it's been screaming
I'll never give up.

(It's been alone.)

(Your heart gave up some time ago now.)

While mine is dying in a war
it does not know how to walk away from.

For You

It is a buoy,
an anchor,
a parachute.

A whisper,
a shout,
a push,
a hand to hold.

It is a love letter,
a goodbye letter,
both,
neither,
it's whatever
you want it
to be.

Go on,
    take it.

I wrote it for you.

What Do You Want from Me

What do you want from me.
They've taken a spatula
to my insides
and scraped out all I had,
and what do you want from me.
My skin, my bones, my muscles.
Want me ripped down to my studs,
want my studs,
want to dig up my foundation.
You don't know how much
you ask of me
every time
you look at me.
I hold up empty arms and let you see
how the wind passes right through me.
What do you want from me.

(Please tell me all you want from me is me.)

What's Left

You didn't take all of it,
but you took enough of it that
I do not know
if I can make anything of
what's left.

The Right Thing

Someday I will find the right thing,

and until then,

I will remind myself

of all the reasons

you

weren't

it.

I Asked the Moon to Dinner

I asked the moon to dinner, but
he said you got him in the breakup.

Fine.

I ask a star, the first star I see tonight, but
she said she's waiting to hear your wishes.

I try the wind, but
it keeps howling your name,
and I think that would make it poor company.

Perhaps the trees, the swaying trees, but
they are still bare, still missing parts of themselves,
still reaching and reaching and reaching.

So, alone it is, I decide, alone it is,
except —

I am with the moon, the star, the wind, the trees.

Yours, and waiting, and howling, and

empty.

Anyway, I Reach

I don't know if I reach because

my hands are empty

or if I reach because

I want you.

Anyway, I reach.

We Just Learn

I don't believe that time heals all wounds.
I think that sometimes
we just learn
to live with
the pain.

Waves

Sadness is almost always
a quiet sea that lives within me,
except for the nights
when the moon tugs a little harder
and turns it
into
waves.

Why

They told me
I couldn't love you anymore,
and I said,
I know,
but tell me why,
but tell me why.

Just like when you said
you didn't love me anymore,
and I said,
I know,
but tell me why,
but tell me why.

(Nobody ever tells me why.)

Never Not

I am never not missing you.
Saying your name where nobody can hear it.
Calling it.
Wailing it.
I am never not where you are.
Although I am here.
Although I am smiling.
I am never not reaching.
Hands in knots,
knuckles white,
I have a lean in me, do you see
this lean in me.

Somebody bought me roses,
and I named each thorn for you.

I keep letting you

make me

bleed.

Cotton

You are one of the four walls of this house.
The sturdiest, the one nobody can get through.
And me, though I was a wrecking ball
in a past life, I cannot help because
in this life, I am more cotton, less wrecking,
soaked in rubbing alcohol and pressed
against wounds
just long enough for the screams
to turn silent.

And the walls stay up.

And I stay inside.

And nobody knows because

the screams

are

silent.

And He Does

He smiles down at me, and I think,
here is the part where he kisses me.
(And he does.)

He kisses me, and I think,
here is the part where he asks me to stay.
(And he does.)

He asks me to stay, and I think,
here is the part where he tells me he loves me.
(And he does.)

He tells me he loves me, and I think,
here is the part where he leaves.
(And
     he
        does.)

Most of the Time

I am sometimes
stretched out along
the full curve of my spine,
sometimes curled up
in the heel of one foot,
sometimes buried
in the back of my throat,
sometimes cowering
within my own heart,
palms pressed
against my ears
so I can't hear
the roil and wail of it.

(Sometimes I am here.)

(Most of the time I am gone.)

And If Not

Look, I want to say,
as he starts walking toward the door,
look —
would it matter if
I told you that
I loved you.

(And if not, why not.)

(And if not, I do not understand how it could not.)

Girl

I am a girl when I laugh,
a woman when I love,
both when I cry.

Girl when I trust,
woman when I leave,
both when I hold on.

I am a girl when I believe you'll come back.

I am a woman when I admit

that I'm better off if

you don't.

Never You

What will hurt the least,
is how I make decisions now.
What carries within it
the lowest potential to inflict pain.
What
    or
        who.
Who sees me whole and doesn't wonder
what I'd look like in pieces.
Whose hands are more glue, less sledgehammer,
more cup, less fist,
more silk, less sandpaper.

Less file.

Less making me less.

What will hurt the least.

(The answer is never you.)

Fix It

The smallest of cracks
can splinter and spread and shatter
if you don't take the time to fix it.

And what I'm saying is,
I don't understand
why you won't take the time
to fix it.

Fingerprinted

I am still working on shedding
this fingerprinted skin,
because none of the prints
are mine.

And I am exhausted by the thumbprint
on the curve of my hip.

And I am drained by those scattered
along the edge of my jaw.

And I am worn by the ones
on the backs of my hands.

And I am afraid that if somebody finds me,
they're not going to know
that I am mine
and not
yours.

Keep Me

I am the approximate size and shape
of a promise,
the width and depth
of forever.

(Nobody can keep me.)

Like Hallelujah

I wrote you a song today,
and it goes something like
small graces and serendipity.

I sing it like a lullaby,
like a ballad,
like hallelujah,
like slow and steady,
like hallelujah.

I sing it to you,
but that doesn't mean
I'm not always hoping
that one day
you'll sing it
to me.

Still

I wish I could say I'm over it but

my head is still beneath it and

I still

can't

breathe.

Roots

Love has roots,
I can't give it all away to you.
It erupts from my chest and
winds through my rib cage and
it took so long to grow here,
no,
I can't give it all away to you.

I pluck seeds from it and
plant them carefully in your chest,
but you always forget
to water them, so
I stay here and remind you and
I let you call me love.

I stay here and remind you and

you let me
    call you
        love.

Blinded

The light is too bright in places,
and by the light I mean you,
and by in places I mean everywhere.
I am more curtains, more blinds,
more wanting less of being blinded,
for nothing is clear
through a squint.
You know how if you stare
into the sun
for long enough,
even when you close your eyes
you'll see the glow?

(That is exactly what I'm afraid of.)

An Echo

You are an echo, now,
long gone,
long gone,
but I hear you,
but I hear you.

Someone reminded me
that I am an echo, too.

Do you hear me,
do you hear me.

I am whispering

                    your name.

Smaller

It took me a long time to learn

that just because

not everyone can hold me,

does not mean

I should ever make myself

smaller.

You Did This

I know

that you didn't mean

to do this,

and I wish that changed

the fact

that you

did this.

That's It

I had a dream that you remembered me.

That's it,
that's the whole poem.

Broken Glass

I have a fight in me,
and nothing civilized like
pistols at dawn, no,
more like a bar fight,
a brawl,
a couple of drunken fools
who think they know
a thing about a thing.
That's the kind of fight
I have in me,
yes, a dirty fight, an ugly fight,
I smash the bottle against the wall
and come at you with
the shards of it,
is how I tell you
not to go,
is how I growl at you
to stay,
I say, fight me, damn you, fight me,
no, I say fight for me, damn you, fight for me,
as your hands stay at your sides,
as you don't look me in the eye,
as you go quietly into the night
and everyone who walks past wonders
why I'm clinging to broken glass.

I Understand

I know that you can stand up,
as surely as I know
that I can.

But I also understand if,
like me,
you'd rather

not

just yet.

The Elephant in the Room

You may have buried the past,
but I dug it back up,
dusted it off,
framed it,
put it on the goddamn mantel.
It's the elephant in the room
I hang my coat on
and lean against when I'm tired.
Everyone knows better
than to ask me about it,
but I tell them about it anyways.
I say, oh that?
Let me tell you about that —

it is hard to be the one left behind.

(There isn't much else to tell.)

Handlebars

Even as a child,
when all of my friends were doing it
and that was a good enough reason
to do just about anything,
I never took my hands off
of my bicycle handlebars.
Why would I willingly relinquish control.
No, I hold tight,
I'm a person who holds tight,
who steers,
I want a say in where I go.
I want
      to pretend
                I have a say in where I go.
(I know I don't really have a say.)
The earth turns, gets picked up
and flipped along its axis,
the road splits into two,
and I try, I try, but in the end —
I go down the one
he
isn't
on.

Better than Nothing

I don't always know
where this sadness comes from,
except to know
it lives within me,
except to know
I am never without it.

Except to know
you gave me some of it.

Except to know
it's all you've let
me keep of you.

(And to know it's better than nothing.)

On My Own

I hoped you would build this life with me,
but I know
that I am so much stronger
for having to build it
on my own.

Into the Fire

I am not so brave; there is only
one time in all of my life
I have run into the fire
when everyone else
was running
out.

(This is all I know of love.)

I Keep Hoping

Look, I've drowned before,
and I don't mean look as though
you have any chance of seeing,
but please just try, just try,
to look.

You are quicksand to me, and
everyone offers me hands and ropes
and branches, but even when my head
is just about to go under, I don't let anybody
save me.

(I keep hoping that you will.)

Can You

Do you think that you could save me.

Not will you, not can you,
just do
you think
you could.

(Then will you.)

(Then can you.)

He's Why

He doesn't hold me like a question,
no, he holds me like an answer.
Not to a question he had about me,
but to a question he's always had about himself.

And I hold him like it all makes sense now.

I hold him like he's why.

A Cure

I have scars on the wrong side
of my skin. I name them like
a warrior names his weapons.
That one is September 2nd and that
one is your smile and that one is
goodbye, I whisper just
loud enough for nobody
to hear, I shout just loud
enough for nobody
to hear because nobody
is anywhere close to near.
They used to bleed
the sick to try to cure them
of disease, and I think that if
you cut me open,
all that would spill out
is you. That is not to say
you are disease. It is just
to say that I carry you
within me. It is just to say
that I am hoping
there's
a cure.

This Still

My heart has aligned itself with
the thunder. I count the seconds between
the pounds, the peals, each one another
mile between us.
When the storm finally ends,
I don't stop counting.
This still, this silence —
it is the true measure of
how far apart we are.

I Lose Things

I lose things.
Everyone knows this about me,
says I'd lose my head
if it wasn't attached at the neck,
probably isn't surprised when I say
I lost you.
It's what I do, and
I'm good at what I do,
I'm great at what I do,
the audience gives me
a standing ovation
when I do what it is I do.
(I lose things.)

But the truth is,
you just can't keep
what doesn't want you.

Tiptoes

I have been on tiptoes, now,
afraid, now,
wanting to run
but hardly brave enough
to walk.
I cannot stand that
I cannot stand
in the face of this.
That fear's name
rolls off the tip of my tongue
but I can never remember
how to pronounce courage.
The irony,
that my courage cowers,
that my courage has no spine.
That my fear roars,
that my fear stands tall.
That my heart stops and starts
and it is only in the stops
that I remember
I'm alive.

A Mess of Things

I have made a mess of things,
or you have made a mess of things,
I don't know, there's just a mess of things,
and we're sitting in its midst.

And I swear I'm speaking,
but you can't hear me.

And I swear I'm listening,
but you aren't speaking.

And I swear, I swear,
that there's a road we haven't found,
one that's wide enough
for you to carry your dreams
and for me to carry my dreams
and for us to be together —
we just need
    to keep
        looking.

To You

I write it all for me,
but I write
it all
to you.

Sunrise

He is a sunrise.

(It has been dark for a long time.)

In Contradictions

I beg you in contradictions.
To stay, to go.
I don't know what I want,
do you know what you want,
do you know what
                    I
                        want.

Yes, I know, I want you.

But I also want you
    not to
        hurt me.

Outstretched

My arms are outstretched,
are always outstretched,
my arms are outstretched toward you.

Reaching for you
when your back is turned.

Keeping you at arm's length
   anytime
      it's not.

Only Because

We sit beneath the weight of our words,
and if they hold us under,
if we can't breathe through them,
if they hurt —

it's only

because

they matter.

(It's only because we mattered.)

The Moon and the Waves

You are the moon,
and I am the waves.

You pull me,
and I climb;

you pull me,
and I climb.

But I could never reach you —

and I was always
    going to
        break.

What I Called Myself

There isn't a word for this.
I know, I've looked, I've tried.
I've tried devastated
and I've tried fine.
Heartbroken
and better,
sad
and full of hope.
I've tried lonely,
content,
lost,
and just to try it,
I've tried found.

None of them fit as well as the days
when what I called myself was

yours.

All or Nothing

And I know I said all or nothing,

I know I said all or nothing,

but I cannot

stand

the nothing.

Stay

This whole time,
I've just been wishing
that you'd love me.

I should have wished
that loving me
would be enough to make you stay.

Just Because

Just because
I've grown accustomed to
not having you,
does not mean
that I don't still want
to have you.

I Fall for You

If you are the wind,
I am the leaves on every tree.

I fall for you.

Miracles

There have been miracles, and

I think

that we

could be one.

Flotsam

These hearts are more wreckage than
ship now, more at the bottom
of the ocean than floating
on top of it, more tear
less hull, more hole
less bow, more forgotten
less stern. These hearts are flotsam where
flotsam can be defined as either
the wreckage of a ship or
things which have been declared
worthless, but while you may think that
beating is to hearts as sailing
is to ships, I have this to say:

hearts beat on even after they've sunk.

Enough Things

I have watched

enough things end

to know

that I don't want this

to be one of those things.

Sometimes

I will say this,
yes,
I will say this,
because you can say things
even if
you're not sure you
believe them —

sometimes love isn't enough.

Bravely

I do not love you fearlessly.

(I am afraid.)

And so I love you

bravely.

I Will Try

I found this in
the charred remains
of all we used to be:

peace.

It isn't quite what I had hoped for,
but it's more than I thought I'd find,
and so —

I will try
to let it
be
enough.

Bones

I have braced bones, ready for impact
bones, been broken before bones, be
careful bones, still want him bones, shouldn't
want him bones, can't help it bones, haunted
bones, hopeful bones, in this for
the long haul bones.

Carved,
      carved,
            carved bones.

(Carved with his name bones.)

Hope is a Pillow

Hope is a pillow, now
hear me out. It is either
a soft place
for my head to rest, or
it is pressing down
over my face.

It is either how I sleep
at night
or the reason
I can't
breathe.

Either way, I carry it with me.

Either way,

I never

set it

down.

Well Enough

I never leave
well enough alone
because what if well enough
could be turned into
amazing.

The Space Between Us

There is an ocean between us,
even though of course there isn't.
Just land, just fields and roads and
I think there's a mountain range and
I'm guessing a river or two, people,
sure, and I bet they're laughing, I bet
they're crying, I bet they're shaking
their fists at the sky and their hands with
the devil and I bet some of them are
laughing, yes I hope some of them are
laughing, and I bet some of them
are in love, yes I hope head over heels,
you know, I hope most of the space
between us is filled with love and laughter.

I would so like for most
of the space in me
to be filled with love and laughter.

But there is an ocean between us,
even though of course there isn't.

(Just rivers.)

(Just mountains.)

Ours

You took your dreams
with you when you left,
and you took my dreams
with you when you left,
and you left me

here with

ours.

Always

They asked what I
still loved about you, you,
gone you, don't know
you, did but don't, can't,
what could I possibly
still love about you.

I said I love
what I've always loved —

your voice where it fills silences.
your smile where it lights darknesses.
every space that is no longer empty because
you
are standing
within it.

I love what I've always loved.

(I love who I've always loved.)

One More Time

How about one more time,
what do you think about one more time.
What do you think about
sunrises, have you given much thought to
springtime, what about phoenixes, do you
think about phoenixes, do you think about
them as fire or do you think about them as
ash. I'm no longer sure where
endings end and beginnings begin,
or if it's all part of the same thing.
If the phoenix is still ash even though
it's now fire.

If it will always be ash, just
where nobody can see it.

Anyway, how about one more time.

What do you think about
    one
        more
            time.

Make Do

I'm not saying I adapt well,
but I adapt. I learn
how to sleep on a wet pillow. I dial
your number but I hang up
before it rings. I wish on airplanes,
on 11:12, on blades of grass if
I can't find a dandelion. I make do
with what I have, I make do with what
I don't have. Because what's the
alternative, no really, what's the alternative,
someone tell me, is there an alternative.

I am doing my best while I'm not
at my best, and I am proud of every
day that I wake up and make do in a world
that you're
not
in.

I Bring Them Back

My hopes have heartbeats,
I keep them alive.
Though some are frail,
I don't give up on them.
They taper, they fade,
I bring them back.
Me, I don't let go,
I won't let go,
okay fine,
I can't let go.

I bring them back.

My hopes, these hopes,
that you'll
be back,
I bring

them

back.

How Far

I stand at the bottom of my driveway
every time, but nobody ever turns around.
I'm always waving, always waiting,
always ready to say
welcome back,
always only saying
come back.
I am always saying it to
the wind.
I am always saying,
how far can you carry these words.

How far.

Can you take them so far away
that I can't hear them anymore,
so far away that
maybe
he
can.

Me and Tink

I sit beside Tinkerbell on a tree trunk
and we talk about unrequited love
while Wendy and Peter dance circles
above us in the air.
I say, "Tink, he's never gonna grow up,
why would you go falling
for a boy like that,"
and she gives me a look.
I say, "Tink, he's always flying off,
always picking fights, you know,
he's always thinking about the next thing,"
and she looks like she's
got something to say,
but she doesn't say it.
I say, "Tink, you've got wings, girl,
you can go anywhere, girl,
love anyone be anyone, you know,
you've got the world at your feet, girl,"
and she shakes her head at me
like I'm a fool, am I a fool,
I don't know, and so I stop talking
and she stops listening
and we watch them dance amongst
the fireflies, and my mind drifts to you,
it floats to you,
and I wonder
when you'll
call.

Looking for You

I am looking for you
under rocks.
I am lifting conversations
and touches and smiles,
looking for you.
I am staring at ceilings
that aren't mine,
looking for you.
I am saying Marco,
listening for Polo,
saying ready or not,
here I come,
looking for you.

I am saying I'm done
looking for you.

But when nobody is looking,
I
  always
            am.

More Flash, Less Boom

I am thunderous in my sadness,
lightning in my joy. I pour rain
all over this town, all over
this town, making everything
green, making everything drown.
Making everything beautiful
just before it dies, like you, kind of like
you. I scare children
with my grief now, didn't you
know. But I also haven't stopped
lighting up the sky with
everything that beats inside of me.

But I also haven't stopped
loving you.

It's just that loving you used to be
more flash,
                less boom.

~~Simply Impossible~~ Impossibly Simple

It is as simple as this:

all I want is you.

And it is as impossible as this:

all

I want

is you.

Avant Garde

Someone tipped me over
and I spilled all of these words,
and I'm sorry for the mess, I say,
I'm sorry for the mess. Put a rope
around them all, no flash
photography, frame them in my bones.

It's art, it's avant garde.

(You can look,
but you can't touch.)

You, who see Van Gogh's
Starry Night
and think you understand
his madness —

know that still,
you have no concept
of his heart.

Firefly

You have firefly eyes;
they flicker in the dark.

   They glow.

A firefly heart to match.

I cup it in my hands.

I put it in a jar.

And it doesn't
   stand
      a chance.

Hold On

I have been reaching
for so long that
I do not know what to do
now that your hand's in mine.

(Hold on, I guess.)

(I think I'm going to hold on.)

Glass

I am very good at this,
have you seen how good I am at this.
People pay money
for my smile,
they buy it,
they raise their eyebrows and
nod at one another, impressed,
lifting their paddles to bid even though
they hadn't thought this would be sold.
But I sell it and
they buy it, yes,
I am very good at this.

You're the only one who knows I'm brittle,
fragile,
glass.

(You're the only one who sees right through me.)

Armchair Heart

I have an armchair heart.

(It gets comfortable.)

People ask if it wants to go
somewhere else, do
something else, I don't know, maybe
love someone else,
but it says no, I'm good.

I'm good here, right here,
more than good, right here,
you know, I've never been anywhere
better than right here.

I have faith
    that he'll
        be back.

(And so I'll wait right here.)

Regrets

I can tell you this about regrets:

whatever you think they weigh,

they

weigh

more.

We Are, We Are

Yes, these shadows, they're
supposed to be there. These
scars, they're supposed to
be there. It's all supposed
to be there, and I'm supposed to
be here, and everything that is,
is as it's meant to be because
it is. And it would not be if
it should not be, do you hear
me, do you hear me. We are here
and we are now and we are, we are,
we are.

(A miracle, I think.)

(We are, we are

a miracle.)

Multitudes

Love will never ask for
more than you have to give.
It will not take
without giving you something in return,
even if that something
looks different than you'd expected.
(Than you'd hoped.)

Love will not leave.

I promise you, I promise you,
                              it will not leave.

It may fold itself up small
and tuck itself away,
but it will not be lessened.

Just because it needs to
take up a little less space for now,
does not mean that later
you won't be able to unfold it
until
it takes up
multitudes.

Forever

I have not yet gone numb.

(I feel it all.)

For better or

for worse or,

I'm starting to fear,

forever.

In the Silence

In the silence,
the sky is falling,
even if it isn't.
Air turns to water,
here turns to gone,
even if it doesn't.
In the silence,
I can't see you,
even if you're there.

And in the silence,
I am less,

even

if

I'm not.

Didn't You See

Don't just stand there, I want to howl.
I want to shove us.
Sometimes closer, sometimes away.

No, I never want away.

I want to say, what the hell is your hand
doing not in his, why is he looking away,
why are you letting him, why aren't you
fighting, why isn't he fighting, why aren't

either of you

fighting.

I want to say, you fools.
Didn't you see what you had.
Didn't you, didn't you see.

Didn't you see that it was beautiful.

Otherwise

When you asked if I was happy,
I thought you meant right here,
right now,
talking to you.

Otherwise,
the answer
would have been
no.

But Then I Think It Can

Love can't conquer all
if we
don't
help it.

Lost

You said that it was hard to lose me,
me, flashing light me, neon sign
saying I'm here me,
calling your name, calling your name,
calling your name me,
and yet,
somehow,
you managed it.

Make Believe

I make believe
that I believe
we can make something
of all of these
ashes.

All the Same

I'm an open book of
I miss you,
a song turned all the way up to eleven of
I want you,
I scrub my face twice a day,
but it's still written all over it,
forehead to chin,
bold,
red,
dripping.

It says,
I know you're not looking, but

I love you

all

the same.

What Do You Give Up

You say you give up,
but what. What do you
give up, do you know exactly what
you're giving up, have you
thought about it, have you really
thought about it, do you know
that the thing you're
giving up is
me.

Say it,
not just
I give up.

Say,
     I give
          you up.

If

If you can live without me,

I think it's better

for both of us

if

you

do.

Eighty Times a Minute

If my heart beats eighty times a minute,
115,000 times a day,
42 million times a year —

anyway, it beats for you.

That's all I wanted to say.

Not Enough

I don't say it aloud,
but I think it,
but I think it —

when you say
you miss me

and

when you say
you want me

and

when you say
you love me —

I don't say it aloud,
but I think it
in the echoes —

(not enough.)

From Love

Sometimes I think I'm
ricocheting beneath my skin
and against my bones,
like I cannot be contained,
like there are bruises all inside of me
from love flailing
from love pulling
from love trying and trying to escape.

(From love trying
                to reach
                        you.)

Your Decision

You can say

that love left,

but it was your decision

to let it

go.

Part Volcano

I am part volcano, I try
so hard not to erupt but then
the lava has nowhere to
go, burns me from the
inside, scalds me, bubbles,
boils, I am blistered just
beneath my skin, though
you wouldn't know, no, I know
you wouldn't know.

You have to want
to know to know, and you —

you have never
    wanted
        to know.

(You have never really known me.)

And I've Tried

This life I've led since you.
I'm flown,
    floated,
        fallen,
and I've laughed,
    loved,
        languished,
and I've sung,
    swam,
        stumbled,
and I've tried
and I've tried
and I've tried,
    thrilled,
        trembled,
and I've moved,
    marveled,
        missed,
okay,
    I've missed,
        yes,
I have lived
    this life
        without you, but
it doesn't mean
    I haven't
        missed you.

Perennial

I am a tulip,
a peony,
a hydrangea.

I may disappear,
but I am only buried,
only hidden,
not gone.

I may need a little time,
but again
and again
and again —

I'll bloom.

A Memory

I run lines with you
in my head, but you go
off-script half the time,
more than half the time,
and me, I'm a terrible
improviser, just awful,
I can't keep up, I say
things like
I love you
right after you say
goodbye.

It's rehearsal,
it's a play.

(But no, but no —)

I know that it's
a memory.

But Still

You know, the sun's gonna rise tomorrow
either way, yeah,
it's gonna set,
moon's gonna climb up into the sky,
the world's gonna keep right on
turning and turning,
babies are gonna be born,
people are gonna live,
gonna die,
gonna fall in love,
hearts are gonna break,
everything's gonna keep happening,
it's all gonna keep happening,
yeah, all of it, all of it,
whether

    or not

you're here.

(But still, you know, I would like you here.)

(I would very much like you here.)

Careful

I am careful.

Even if

I'm holding onto

nothing,

I

don't want

to break it.

Treading Water

I am treading water, not
drowning, not swimming,
not going anywhere, no,
not going anywhere, just
keeping my head up above
it all, not sure how far I am
from shore, not sure how
much longer I can do this,
how much longer I'll have
to do this, if it will
at some point
be worth it.

I'm not sure if any of this is worth it.

But just in case,
I'm going

to stay

right here.

Do You Remember

Do you remember when
I'd lean against you,
when I needed somewhere to lean?
That was before I climbed up into you
to hide from the world
and before I inched out
onto limbs that turned
to branches that turned
to twigs, just trying to see
a little slice of blue skies,
and before you snapped
and before I fell
and before I broke
every
little
piece
of my heart.

(Do you remember?)

I Have Missed You

It's late now,
and you're asleep beside me.

I want to wake you up and tell you,
but I will write it here instead —

I have missed you,
I have missed you,
I have missed you.

Be Brave

I have a "stay"
in the back of my throat,
which is kind of like a tickle except
it burns, kind of like a tickle except
I can't clear it away, can't swallow
it down, can't do anything
with it, really,
except,
perhaps,
say it.

(Except, perhaps, be brave and say it.)

All of Them

I make you promises, I say

you have my word,

but really what I mean is

you have

all

my words.

I Climbed

Sometimes it's
a mountain I climbed,
and sometimes it's
a pit I climbed up out of.

Either way —

I climbed.

Listening

It is hard
to keep listening
when there's never anything
to hear.

It Takes Two

It takes two to hold tight
to love,
and, you know,
I think
it takes two
to let it
go.

Eulogy

I'll be honest, some days this is
less poem, more eulogy. Do you
see it in the words, do you feel
the way I am waiting for you to say
I'm sorry for your loss
so I can say
there was nothing anyone could do.
Do you believe it when
I say it, do I say it like
I mean it.

Tell me, do I tell
a convincing lie.

I toss dirt down into
the grave, even though
the coffin's empty.

(There wasn't anything left to bury.)

Already Broken

The heart wants
what it wants, trust me,
I know. It's like a child
in the grocery store checkout line,
digging in its heels,
howling,
refusing to listen to reason,
refusing to relinquish its hold
on the thing that it wants,
needs,
has to have,
swearing it won't
break it.

I don't know how to tell it
that the thing it wants
is already
broken.

I Need You

Some days I
am a little more soaked in gasoline,
and your hands
are a little more flame,
and I know that it makes no sense,
but on those days —

I need you
   to hold me
      a little
         more tightly.

Masochist

I am a try again, a can we get a
do-over, a yes that hurt
last time but maybe
this time it will not. Kind of a
masochist, I guess you could
say, some people say, I have said
before. I touch the paint to see
if it's dry, but even if it's not,
I say it's ready. Go ahead, do
your worst, I mean, do your
best, I mean, let's see what
we are made of. Maybe we are
still made of exactly what
we were made of then, but maybe
we're made of
more, better, best.

So go ahead, do your best.

(Love me this time.)

More Everything

I am more fall than
winter, more spring
than fall, more
summer than anything.
You are all blue skies
and windows down,
radio up so high I can't
hear you singing along, but
I know you are and
I know I am and
I know I've felt like this
before, it's just
I never knew I could feel it again.

I am more summer than anything, yes,
but we —

we are more everything
than it all.

Ever

You think you hear the ghost of
                    yet
behind the things I say like
I'm not going anywhere and
I don't want anyone else and
I'm not going to stop loving you.

But you're hearing wrong,
you're hearing wrong.

(It's really the ghost of
                    ever.)

The Answer

I have chosen you
over and over and
over again, like the
universe keeps asking me
this question, keeps
trying to catch me
off guard, keeps trying to
trick me into giving
another answer,
any other answer, but
can't it see
I'm looking up,
can't it see
I'm cheating?

(The answer is written in the stars.)

(The answer is only ever gonna be you.)

Harbor

I am an exposed nerve, raw
edges, the point where
two ends of a battery that
are never supposed to touch
meet.

I harbor sparks, you know,
ships, possibly,
maybe a grudge or two,
and I harbor
one
great love.

And so in case, just
in case, on the very off
chance you were wondering —

if you had asked,
I would have
said yes.

Flags

Dawn breaks, and so
do we. You keep waving
flags, and I cannot tell if
they're white or red, but
either way, it's time
for me to go. Past
time. Past tense. It was
time for me to go. It has been
time for me to go
for quite some time now, but,
you know, only one
of your hands
is holding any flags.

(The other is holding mine.)

Maybe This

I am wrapped in sheets
of faith, a tangible thing,
clutched against my body
with desperate arms and
fingertips and elbows, with
pleading, yes, with trembling
hope /
      belief /
            conviction —

maybe this

will be

the thing

that saves me.

I Just Live

I do not live
for this or
because of this or
in spite of this.

I just live and this
is part of me.

I just live and I

am part

of this.

Beneath the Weeping Willow

I have taken to sitting
beneath the weeping willow
every time I want to cry.
(It's nice to be understood.)
I ask her what she's crying over,
and she says okay so,
it's springtime now,
but winter's gonna come,
my leaves are gonna fall,
I don't know if I'll survive it.
I say, why are you crying about
something you can't do
anything about, why aren't you
soaking in the sunshine, why
aren't you living while the living's good.
She said fine then,
what are you crying about
down there, and I say, well,
I'm scared that someday
he's gonna change his mind and
leave. She didn't have to say
anything, you know, I heard it when
I said it. She didn't have to say anything,
and she didn't. We just cried
a little more together, but this time
I think some of it was because of
how beautiful it is that
she's in love with springtime and
how beautiful it is that
I'm
in love
with you.

I Grow Old Here

I grow old here. My roots
wrap themselves around
immovable things like
cement and steel and
hope. Some people mistake
my bared teeth for a smile
because they don't want
to have to ask
why I've bitten off so
much pain. I wish they would,
if only so I could tell them
that it did not taste like pain
at the moment when I bit it.
No, it was sweet once, but
now I grow old here. I am
a reaching thing, like a toddler
who had grown accustomed to
being picked up and now is trying
to find the strength in her own legs
when she does not does not
want to.

Anyway, I've said it before, I know,
but I grow old here.

I do not mind it; I just thought
you might have liked
to grow old here with me.

Orpheus

You ask me
what I want to talk about,
and I say, you know what,
it makes me crazy that
Orpheus looked back,
you know, it makes me absolutely
crazy that he made it all the way
to the Underworld, convinced Hades
to return to him his love, and all
he had to do, the only thing he had to do,
was not look back,
do you think it was a matter of
trust, do you think it was
a matter of doubt, you know,
it makes me crazy, and
you stop me there and you say
okay,
you say,
okay,
tell me what you really
want to talk about.

I say,
I don't know how to not look back.

I say,
I'm scared
      you won't
           be there.

Not Allowed

You are not allowed
to miss me
because I am right here
and you are choosing
not to
have me.

Insurrection

This is mutiny, here, not something
romantic, no, just insurrection, a
revolution, a pistol pointed at the sky
like the sky doesn't feel any pain.

It is bleeding blue, swimming,
swam, swum through and through
with falling things like
asteroids and stars and bullets.

I stand in a crater
the approximate depth of
my broken heart.

Which is to say, I've fallen through —

floating up above it all
beside the asteroids and stars and bullets.

(Struck and struck again.)

Kairos and Chronos

I fall in love with Kairos
but marry Chronos because I'm
a fool. I fall to the ground at my love's
feet and say, forgive me, I plead,
forgive me, but all he asks is *why*.
It isn't enough for me to say that
I'm a fool, and so I think it through —
I lift my hands like I'm a scale, though my
hands are empty. Time is falling faster
than I can catch it, I tell him. Somebody said
should, and I thought that maybe
they were right. He shakes his head
and says I'm right, that I'm
a fool.

I have waited all of my life
to catch a star inside my hands,
but, impatient, I settle for
a firefly.

And it's already flickering.

And it's already dying.

While stars fall all around me.

(While stars fall all around me.)

Proud

Somebody once told me that
the strength is in never
letting them see how much they've
hurt you, but no, I think the strength
is in letting them see how much
you cared.

Instead of sheep I count the times
I put my heart out in the world,
small and bruised and fragile.

(I fall asleep proud.)

You and Me

If any-
thing
in this
world
has ever
been meant
to be,
I swear
to god
it's you
and me.

Origin Story

I was standing there,

holding heartbreak in my hands,

and I did not know what

to do with it.

(So I wrote it down.)

CONTENTS

ACKNOWLEDGMENTS

For the boy I met at closing time
at a bar nearly seven years ago.

You know all of these poems are about you.

(Cover design by Maialen Alonso.)

ABOUT THE AUTHOR

Kristina Mahr devotes her days to numbers and her nights to words. She works full-time as an accountant in the suburbs of Chicago, where she lives with her two dogs and two cats, but her true passion is writing. In her spare time, she enjoys spending time with her family and friends, reading, and waking up at the crack of dawn every weekend to watch the Premier League.

You can find more information about her other poetry collections, *It's Only Words* and *I Wrote You a Poem*, as well as her fiction novels, on her website at:

www.kristinamahr.com

52105945R00142

Made in the USA
San Bernardino, CA
05 September 2019